Tell the Truth.
Make It Matter.

a memoir writing workbook

Beth Kephart
National Book Award Finalist

Illustrations by: William Sulit

Copyright © 2017 by Beth Kephart and William Sulit.
All rights reserved. No part of this book may be reproduced
in any form without written permission from the authors.

Printed in USA

What are we supposed to do with that lovely, infuriating, instigating, mischievous blank page?

•

Who are we, when we're being uncommonly honest?

•

Where do we stand, in the landscape of truth?

•

How do we discover and profess the story of our life when lives are such strange and messy things? Frankly, why bother?

In *Tell the Truth. Make It Matter.*, Beth Kephart offers an insider's look at the making of true tales—and an illustrated workbook to guide the wild ride. Combining smartly selected samples with abundantly fresh ideas, dozens of original exercises with cautions, questions with answers, Kephart inspires, encourages, and persistently believes in those with a story to tell.

Write this, *Truth* says. Read this. Consider this. Discover who you are. Have some honest fun with words.

CONTENTS

Introduction	8

I. Nothing but the Truth

Seriously?	13
Masquerades	19

II. This Is Your Voice

The Sound of Truth	28
Telling Details	37
Are You Past or Are You Present?	44
Searching for New in the Land of the True	50
Fine Writing Versus Plain Prose	57
Expectations	61

III. The True You

Finding Yourself:	69
How do you ... ?	70
What do you know ... ?	71
Why can't you ... ?	72
What kinds of ... ?	73
Where were you when ... ?	74
What do you believe ... ?	75
On the Hunt for Memory	76
First Memory	87
Critical Junctures	90
Fail Me Now	99

IV. Navigating Your World

Homeward Bound	106
Dinner Is Served	117
Here and Back and Here Again	125
We Need Some Landscape	131
Weatherized	136

V. There Are People Out There

People Who Need People	145
Not My Jawn	158
Personalities	168

VI. Darkroom

Take a Picture	177

VII. Writing Your Memoir

It's Not (Just) About You	186
Write Your Prologue	195
The Story Continues	201

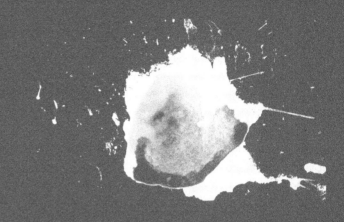

INTRODUCTION

THERE ARE PLENTY OF WAYS TO TELL THE STORY OF YOUR LIFE: As a sharpen-the-pencils science-y report spanning the first thing you remember straight through to the last thing you remember, including this very moment, now. I mean: Now. Actually: *Now*.

(Imagine how long that would take.)

(Imagine how finally impossible.)

As a blow-by-blow of a single something—a single day, a single hour, a single bowling party, a single manicure, a single argument, a single snack, a single shopping spree, a single accident—told precisely as that something happened. Maybe there are possibilities here, but I shall sound the warning bell: You can fool yourself into thinking that simply writing that single something automatically qualifies as meaningful story.

(The bell has rung: It does not.)

As a meditation on the stuff that has—for some reason you'll only discover while writing it down—mattered most. The clinking of your grandmother's knitting needles. The faded flowers that fall from your shelf of antique hats. Your white rat, Joseph, and his quick-tailed genius. Your preference for the color bistre brown. Your obsession with artichokes. Your favorite nook in the library. Your history of love. Your father's talent for burning toast. The smell of sawdust in the garage. Your hoverboard triumphs. The sister you lost. The sister you never had. The sister you always wished you had.

(Now we're getting somewhere.)

As a poem, as a song, as a monologue. As a first-person telling, as a second or a third. As a past-tense rendition or a present-tense sprawl. As a bit of film. As performance art. As a sculpture built of clay. As a cartoon strip.

Yes.

(The thing is: We have options here. Don't let anybody tell you that we don't.)

As a lie, as a distortion, as an attack, as a fiction.

Nope.

(The story of your life is the story of a truth. We don't have options like *that*.)

You're holding a book called *Tell the Truth. Make It Matter*. There's got to be a reason for that. Maybe your aunt read your diary and thought you had the writing knack (have you forgiven her yet?). Maybe homework is due—the kind in which writing is involved—and you're stuck. Maybe you're on vacation in a log cabin with some extra wick in your candlesticks, or maybe you're waiting, in a hospital, for someone you love to get well, or maybe you've just finished reading the best graphic memoir ever and want to know how the author had the courage to tell a story just like that.

Whatever your reasons, truth is now our quest. How we find it, how we share it, how we allow the act of writing our stories to shape our perceptions of ourselves. It's a journey, and you've shown up. You're here. Sharpen your pencils, uncap your pens, click in. Over the course of the coming pages, with the help of leading questions, open-ended prompts, exhortations, and examples, you'll discover your voice, profess the true you, navigate your world, come to know your stories, and write the opening pages (and many scenes) of your memoir. You'll go back in time and lean forward, into the future. You'll study photographs and yield to songs. You'll declare what you know, overcome what you've forgotten, move away from anecdote toward meaning.

I've taught memoir in university classrooms and across the country for years. I've published six memoirs and a book of memoiristic essays. I blog the truth. I interview memoirists. I teach memoir on a farm, by the sea, near a river. I believe, in other words, in memoir. I love the form. But I also know that memoir writing is rarely easy and that we shouldn't expect it to be. This is life that we're talking about it. The wonder and confusion of it. The glories and contradictions. The triumphant and the tragic. The hard-core facts and gauzy dreams.

We've made room for it all in the pages to come.

NOTHING BUT THE TRUTH

TELL THE TRUTH. MAKE IT MATTER.

SERIOUSLY?

Why bother? And what is truth anyway? Aren't we all pretty clear, in this day and age, that the truth is suspect territory? Science keeps outrunning itself. Facts are relentlessly broken. There are lost memories, reconfigured memories, tangled memories, tainted memories, rebuffed memories, and at least a handful of mice at the RIKEN-MIT Center for Neural Circuit Genetics at the Massachusetts Institute of Technology with scientifically induced false memories, according to a *New York Times* story. There's that boy you thought you maybe loved who isn't at all the guy he'd seemed. There's that stranger you saw driving a pickup truck who turned out to be driving a Jeep. There's what your mother said versus what your father said versus what you thought you saw for yourself versus what you told your friend versus what that friend then told your sister.

Truth—be honest—is hard. Memory often falters. My version is not your version. What you leave out (and, as has been seen, we must leave most of it out) is its own kind of contortion. Given the grand impossibility of it all, why rumble down the road in search of truth? Since everything looks like shades of gray, how can any little lie you tell finally make a difference? Who, after all, is going to find out? And how do we make the stories of our lives engaging—how do we deal with that make-it-matter stuff—if, in the end, we are not allowed to bend?

I feel the urge to apologize, but I can't. True stories are life stories, artfully (and honestly) resurrected. They are one person's story—with an eye toward universal consequence. It is the writer speaking not just of himself but of the human condition. It is Big Stuff, or it should be. It can reach across the great divide—connecting people, inspiring people, sometimes even saving people.

It can't do any of that if it springs from deliberate deceit.

I've dared to write six books that fall into the category known as memoir, not to mention what (embarrassingly) now numbers hundreds upon hundreds of truth-infused essays. I've gotten things wrong; believe me, I have. But I've never gotten things wrong *intentionally*. I've never ratcheted up the facts of my story to make me sound more interesting or someone else more dull, me more heroic and someone else less so. I've always done the research, if research was to be done—checked the files, studied the photographs, looked up the old newspaper accounts, talked to the other eyewitnesses.

Because when you commit to telling the truth on the page, you are committing to seeing the world—and yourself—with heroic clarity. He may not be the villain you thought he was. You may not be entirely to blame. What might have seemed like purposeful cruelty at first was really (we learn as we remember, and as we find words for our remembering) an epic misunderstanding. Search for the truth, write that truth, and you grow wiser, more thoughtful, more ready for the world as it is. Search for the truth, and write that truth, and you're not just putting words on a page. You're shaping your own sense of who you are and what you're capable of.

Heroic clarity.

I find it surprising how eager some "truth" writers are to manipulate, or break, the truth. It didn't really happen quite like that, they wink, but the fiction is seducing. It wasn't winter when it occurred, but summer tastes far sweeter. I will change her name and every single thing about her, so that she can't come after me, complaining. She was sipping tea, but for this scene beside that window, I prefer a sugar-free soda.

Small stuff? Inconsequential? Except: It really isn't. Don't mess yourself up by changing the details on purpose. This is *your* life. This is *your* book. Write the truth. Get even the smallest details right. The car he drove. The horse's color. The size of the caterpillar. Choose to write it wrong, lie on purpose, and you punch a hole in your true-story dike. You get a little gush of fiction flowing, and pretty soon anything goes—the lines blur, the facts dim, the message muddies, your testimony is unreliable. Give yourself permission to fabricate one little thing—for the sake of being cool, for the sake of having it easy—and you've stepped across the line.

Don't give yourself permission.

Stand straight.

Be the place where the truth tries to live, because the truth—your best rendering of it, your most honest try—is, in the end, what defines you.

Your truth is your story.

YOUR FIRST LIE

EXERCISE

———

Might as well begin by writing eight full sentences about the first lie you remember ever telling.

Your first lie. Written true:

1.

2.

3.

4.

5.

6.

7.

8.

TIP: *Are your sentences alluring? Do your details sing? If you read these sentences aloud and a pencil dropped, would the whole room hear it? Ask yourself whether there's a bigger story here. A story about a family. A story about a need. A story about who you were before you became the person who chose to tell the lie (had to tell the lie?) you just described. Ask yourself what might have happened if you'd opted for the truth.*

MASQUERADES

Perhaps that wasn't entirely fair—to get you writing the truth by writing about a lie. The fabled cruelty of the blank page is no fable; trust me, I know. The blank page startles. It's like a bottomless lake beneath the shimmer of snow. Sometimes, staring down at it, we see nothing but the crusty white.

So here's a trick of the trade: Tiptoe toward the writing of truth by writing a little bit of fiction. I'm talking warm-up exercises here, not final product. I'm talking about giving yourself a little breathing room.

Turn the page. See what I mean.

FOUND OBJECT

EXERCISE

―――――

Grab the bag or pouch or container that's closest to you. That backpack. That purse. That suitcase. That briefcase. You can even use that old shoebox. Reach in and clutch the first thing your fingers find. Bring it to the light. An old penny? A receipt? A stubby pencil? A barrette? A used-up tube of toothpaste? A feather? A stone? Hold that object. Consider it. Imagine the life it has lived.

How has it felt to be rattling around in the bottom of that purse? How has it felt to be neglected? What secrets does your object know that you have never tried to imagine?

Now write its story using the first-person "I."

BEDROOM DOOR

EXERCISE

Write the story of the door to your bedroom. It's the door that's talking here about what it has seen and what it has felt, what it knows that maybe you have forgotten. (Someone kicked it once. Someone slammed it. Someone plastered it with posters. Someone locked it. Someone broke the lock.)

Something happened.

TIP: *Since it's that door and not you who is talking here, allow that door to speak. Really speak. Is it angry? Moody? Sullen? Afraid? Is it explosive with a secret? I'm listening.*

MOST PRIVATE PLACE
EXERCISE

Write the story of your jewelry box, your treasure chest, your locker—your most private place—in that first-person "I." It's the private place that tells the story. Fill the page with its words.

TIP: *By writing in the voice of something that is not you, you (ironic as it seems) force yourself from the shadows.*

THIS IS YOUR VOICE

THE SOUND OF TRUTH

You've survived. You're back. I suspect that by remembering a lie and writing a bit of fiction you've glimpsed the truth. How that found thing sees you. How that door feels about your life. How your private place waits for the person it knows you are.

Maybe that blank page didn't seem quite so blank, and the writing came quick. Maybe you found, as you wrote, a suite of voices. Maybe by imagining yourself to be something near-to-but-not-you, you (re-)discovered your own authority, your own wit, a touch of your own ambition. Because (unless you skipped that part) you have given the object, the door, and that secret space a language that could have only come from you. You have given them jive, perhaps, or humor, or tenderness, or intelligence, tempo, and metaphor. You have given them a point of view, an attitude, a way of speaking, a history.

A voice.

Memoir is a true story of universal consequence. It is what we find out about what we thought we knew. It is how we see the familiar new. It cannot be told without a voice. And voice is not just the medium with which your story gets told. Voice shapes the story itself. A quiet, metaphorical voice, for example, makes room for reflection, tangents, and introspection. An assertive voice declares and pronounces. A voice that requires a lot of white space is a voice that is pausing, collecting itself, while a voice that jams the pages with long sentences and breathless paragraphs is a voice eager to rip through the tale. What you put into your story and what you take out will be greatly influenced by your voice.

What will the voice of your memoir be? Questing? Defiant? Idiosyncratic? Elaborate? Contemporary? Hopeful? Coy? Slaying? It's too soon to tell, of course. But you've just shown a bit of your style on the page, a little bit of your strut, your lyric, your approach. That makes this the precisely right time to move from fiction to truth.

Return to the work you just completed. Underline the details that speak as much of or for you as they do for the object, the door, and the place. Without losing any of the vulnerability or sass or wisdom you've just mastered by imagining yourself as something you are not, tell us something first-person true about you.

FOUND OBJECT

EXERCISE

That thing you found in the bottom of the purse spoke through you.

But now it is time to speak for yourself. Using the details you summoned in the first found-object exercise, write a story that is true, a first-person story that happened to you.

THIS IS YOUR VOICE

BEDROOM DOOR

EXERCISE

By giving your bedroom door room to speak for itself, you unlocked some measure of your own past.

Now write the story of what happened near or to or because of that door, using your own voice and some of your best found details.

TIP: *"Memoir shapes and crafts the story in such a way that someone else can enter the world, carry it with them. That, to me, is a beautiful and generous act."* — Chloe Honum

MOST PRIVATE PLACE

EXERCISE

Your secrets live in every corner of your world. By writing about your treasure box or your private closet or the felt pouch inside your jewelry box, you've located a secret or two.

Now write the story of that secret in your own first-person I.

TIP: *"If we're going to make it, we have to look at the fear."* — Megan Stielstra, The Wrong Way to Save Your Life

TELL THE TRUTH. MAKE IT MATTER.

TELLING DETAILS

It's the red bird in a dark forest. The black sock in the white laundry basket. The cat with the tail dipped in neon paint. The kid playing the guitar in a roomfullof trombonists. The friend with only half of her lip gloss applied. The wallet that has been left behind. The misplaced set of keys.

These things stand out. Why? What do they mean? How can your mastery of telling details strengthen your memoirist voice?

We are surrounded by *things* in this life. We would be overcome if, for example, someone told us to write down every single thing in the room (or park, or bus, or subway station, or alley way) where we are sitting. We'd have to describe the walls or earth or trash cans, the velocity or stillness, the colors and the smells, the minor objects and the major landmarks, and, of course, ourselves, which is to say our bones, our blood, our skin, our shoes, our clothes, our hair, our hands, the pen in our hands, this book itself.

Writing it all is not just an impossibility. It is (most of the time, though the very rare occasional writer—Karl Ove Knausgaard, say—proves this theory wrong) meaningless. It's the telling details that we're after.

You'll have plenty of room, in the pages that follow, to call up telling details from your own remembered history. But right now, to further know and strengthen your memoir voice, I have prepared some general exercises for you.

Notice what you notice. See what and how you see. Apply your voice to the world beyond yourself.

WHAT DO YOU SEE?
EXERCISE

Spend time with this photograph. Write a single sentence about each of the three most significant details you find. Why does each chosen detail resonate with you?

TIP: *Consider what falls just outside the frame. Consider what might be at work inside the shadows.*

WHAT DO YOU SEE, REDUX?
EXERCISE

Study this illustration. Write a single sentence about each of the three most significant details you find. Take some time, as you work, to understand why you find those particular details to be significant. What does your chosen focus teach you about yourself?

TIP: *If you find yourself obsessed with the negative spaces, stop and ask yourself why.*

WHAT DO YOU SEE NOW?
EXERCISE

Wherever you are at this moment in time, look up. Identify three details that seem to tell a larger story about this current space and your relationship to it. Write those details so spectacularly well that anyone could see them—and know what they mean to you.

TIP: *It's never just about what we see. It's about how we see what we see.*

ARE YOU PAST OR ARE YOU PRESENT?

I was standing there, in the crowd, when it happened—when the line was laid down between Before and After. I noticed the birds first—a big black cloud of them, flying—and then the black cloud suddenly ruptured. I felt the wind through my hair—a fast-moving breeze. I heard somebody say, It's coming, but I didn't know what it was, I couldn't have known what it meant, I couldn't imagine that it would lead us here.

Or:

I'm here. I'm right here, and you're with me, your hand is in my hand, your scruffy cheek is so close I could kiss it, you have that funny cap on, the one I bought you. I look up before you do. I see the birds that look like a cloud—how black they are, how many, how strange. And then I hear someone saying, It's coming. Is it you, saying, It's coming? I look at you. I don't know what you mean.

Where do you stand in relationship to your story? In the past? In the present? With which slice of time do you feel the greatest kinship, and why?

If you rely on the past tense to tell your story, you are giving yourself distance from the events themselves. You are, quite obviously, thinking back. Thinking back to what happened. Thinking back to what it means. Thinking back with a Before-and-After stance. Past tense allows you to foreshadow what is about to come. It allows you to be wise, to have learned your lesson from the scene or moment. It gives you room to come up with a lingering metaphor. It makes it possible to tell an ever-bigger story.

If, on the other hand, you rely on the present tense to tell your story, you are probably keen on urgency. You want to put your readers right there, beside you, as the events or feelings unfold. No filter for you. No distance. Just a heart-pounding it's coming, I don't know what the next minute is, nor do you, my dear readers.

Live this with me, you present-tensers say.

Of course, you are allowed to go both ways—to use both tenses (or, indeed, other tenses such as the future perfect or the past perfect continuous) to tell your story. Don't go random with this. Every tense choice must be deliberate. Tense accidents are going to be obvious ("I see her and I said..."). They're messy ("I hated green apples and I stand up."). They damage your authority.

How do you know which tense is right for the story you hope to tell? The answer is that you can't know until you experiment. Until you write a few paragraphs headed in one direction and then a few paragraphs headed in another. If you're really interested in getting your stories right, you won't simply be changing "said" to "say" or "hated" to "hate." You'll be fully exploring the possibilities that inhere in the ruminative past tense or the urgent present.

Again: Every choice we make in telling our true stories—and in refining our voices—both opens doors and limits us. Every choice must be deliberate. Are you seeking reflective distance or immediacy? Do you want to lay out the facts or explore the feelings? How can you use the majesty of tenses to get closest to the heart of your story?

DISAPPOINTMENT IN THE PRESENT
EXERCISE

Write the story of a major disappointment—something you'd hoped for that just didn't happen. Render it in present tense. Make this scene urgent and alive. Open the door. Let me in.

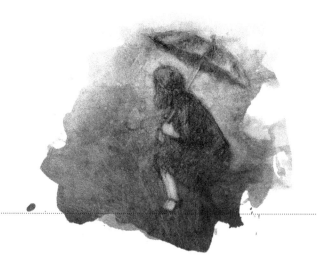

TIP: *A hope inflates. A failure crushes. What words do you have for that? What immediate language?*

DISAPPOINTMENT IN THE PAST

EXERCISE

Write the same story in past tense. Don't just change the tenses. Re-remember. Make this scene reflective, wise. What new details do you discover? What new meaning within those details?

TIP: *"Memoir is the blueprint of a journey, a memory palace, a deep tunneling into the mountain of all that would otherwise be lost." — Brian Turner*

SEARCHING FOR NEW IN THE LAND OF THE TRUE

The writers of our best true stories are philosophers, risk takers, sentence forgers, structural innovators, language shapers. They alert us, calm us, and reach toward us. They say (they imply), *Yes, I have hoped, and yes, I have wanted, and I know that you have, too.*

The best of them do it in their own unique way. Joan Wickersham wrote *The Suicide Index*, about her father's death, by framing her story as, well, an index. Here's a snapshot of the table of contents:

Suicide:
    act of
        attempt to imagine, 1-4
        bare-bones account, 5-6
        immediate aftermath, 734
    anger about, 35
    attitude toward
        his, 36-42
        mine, 43

Ander Monson in *Letter to a Future Lover: Marginalia, Errata, Secrets, Inscriptions, and Other Ephemera Found in Libraries* relies on everything he lists in his subtitle to prompt true stories of discovery, history, or personal shame. Stephanie LaCava in *An Extraordinary Theory of Objects: A Memoir of an Outsider in Paris* relies on objects—poison arrow tree frogs, a skeleton key, a metal pencil case, a curved whale's tooth—to tell the story of that time when her family moved to Paris and she felt stranded. Roz Chast in *Can't We Talk About Something More Pleasant?* and Alison Bechdel in *Fun Home* and Cece Bell in *El Deafo* and Dominique Goblet in *Pretending is Lying* and Kristen Radtke in *Imagine Wanting Only This* rely on drawings and (sometimes) photographs to tell their stories. Mark Richard, in *House of Prayer No. 2*, tells (almost) his entire life story as a "challenged" child growing up in the South in second person. Edward Hirsch tells the story of his adopted son—and the death of that son—in a book-long memoiristic poem called, simply, *Gabriel*.

Truth is a raw and quivering thing. It can assume many forms, take on many shapes, speak through different voices. Don't assume, as you are setting off here, that you are locked into a first-person telling. You are not. There is freedom in that.

POEM IT

EXERCISE

Return to your present-tense disappointment story. Now write it as a poem in second person.

Now write it as a poem in third person.

What do you learn about your story in the process? What do you learn about your voice?

TIP: *The facts remain. The sentences change. When the sentences change, so does the meaning. How many truths? the memoirist asks. How many true versions?*

CARTOON IT
EXERCISE

Return to your past-tense disappointment story. Now draw it as a cartoon. What do you learn about your story in the process? What do you learn about your voice?

TIP: *"In my work I've often used images to convey emotion and words to convey arguments and ideas, but I'm trying to uproot that, too. For me, the most interesting thing about working with text and image is navigating the relationship between the two and figuring out how they can work together (or against) each other."* — Kristen Radtke

TELL THE TRUTH. MAKE IT MATTER.

FINE WRITING VERSUS PLAIN PROSE

In *Living by Fiction*, the great memoirist, essayist, and fiction writer Annie Dillard delineates between fine writing and plain prose in the following fashion:

> Fine writing, with its elaborated imagery and powerful rhythms, has the beauty of both complexity and grandeur. It also has as its distinction a magnificent power to penetrate. It can penetrate precisely because, and only because, it lays no claim to precision. It is an energy. It sacrifices perfect control to the ambition to mean. ... Fine writing is not a mirror, not a window, not a document, not a surgical tool. It is an artifact and an achievement; it is at once an exploratory craft and the planet it attains; it is a testimony to the possibility of the beauty and penetration of written language.

> The prose is, above all, clean. It is sparing in its use of adjectives and adverbs; it avoids relative clauses and fancy punctuation; it forswears exotic lexicons and attention-getting verbs; it eschews splendid metaphors and cultured allusions. ... There is nothing relaxed about the pace of this prose; it is as restricted and taut as the pace of lyric poetry. The short sentences of plain prose have a good deal of blank space around them, as lines of lyric poetry do, and even as the abrupt utterances of Beckett characters do. They erupt against a backdrop of silence. These sentences are—in an extreme form of plain writing—objects themselves, objects which invite inspection and which flaunt their simplicity.

Dillard's categories naturally lead us toward the following exercise.

ARE YOU FINE OR PLAIN?

EXERCISE

Look back on the pages you have written so far. Self-diagnose. Are you a fine writer or a plain proser? Whatever you naturally tend toward, reverse it. If you are a natural fine writer, write a paragraph or two in plain prose. If you are a natural plain proser, write a paragraph or two as a fine writer. Then ask yourself how this exercise deepens the range of your voice.

TIP: *You're on a journey. You need to keep watch over your own progress.*

TELL THE TRUTH. MAKE IT MATTER.

EXPECTATIONS

———

We often expect big things from those who write for us—from the memoirs we read, from the stories we're told, from the books of truth in progress.

But what do we mean by that word, *expect*?

And what do we expect from ourselves?

It's a question I require my University of Pennsylvania Creative Nonfiction students to answer. A conversation we very deliberately have. What do you expect of the writers you read, I ask them, and what do you expect of yourselves? Against which yardsticks will you measure your own work? What do you demand from yourself?

"Put into words the rhythm of my heartbeat—or the things my heart beats for," Silvia asked, of writers. "I expect no less than a beautiful hangover," wrote Dani. Don't tell us everything, David wrote. "Just isolate one lovely shell, a conch of wisdom." Wrote Nina, "I want writers who communicate compexity through flaws, within failures."

And then these writers, my students, asked themselves to deliver the same powerful beats, slivers, truths upon their own pages.

We've reached the end of our voice chapter. We're about to get into the depths of you. Why not pause here and answer these questions yourself? Think of your expectations as touchstones stuff. The frame within which you'll work.

EXPECT BIG THINGS

EXERCISE

Write three paragraphs detailing the expectations you have of the writers you read.

TIP: *If you don't bring an analytical eye to the work of others, you will not be able to bring it to your own work. Every writer needs to know the difference between good and bad, in memoir.*

SET THE BAR HIGH

EXERCISE

Write three paragraphs detailing the expectations you have of your truth-writing self.

TIP: *Don't give yourself an easy exit. Expect of yourself that which you believe you are ultimately capable of. Then raise the bar a little higher.*

THE TRUE YOU

FINDING YOURSELF

You've told the story of a lie. You've masqueraded. You've experimented with, listened to, strengthened your voice.

Now it's time to discover the true you.

To go back into time and deep within yourself.

I have some questions for you. Answer those that resonate. Those that teach you something meaningful about who and what you are.

But don't stop with the questions I've provided. There's more to living than that. Maybe you should be interrogating yourself about wonder and awe—what the words mean and why they matter. Or maybe your current obsession is time, and how it is stopped, held, measured.

Or maybe what you need to know about yourself right now is all bound up in the rules of love. If there are any rules. If there should be.

Your true story is a question waiting to be answered.

Take the time to find the answers.

HOW DO YOU...?

How do you brush your teeth?

How do you slice your bread?

How do you shelve your books?

How do you speak?

How do you perform?

How do you wait?

How do you fight?

How do you hope?

How do you give thanks?

WHAT DO YOU KNOW…?

What do you know about ice?

What do you know about umbrellas?

What do you know about chocolate?

What do you know about luck?

What do you know about wealth?

What do you know about evil?

What do you know about generosity?

What do you know about possibilities?

TIP: *Maybe what you know about umbrellas is that they always break in a storm. Or maybe, beneath umbrellas, you find love. Or maybe you remember an umbrella from a movie, years ago. Maybe umbrellas taught you to dance.*

WHY CAN'T YOU...?

Why can't you eat_____?

Why can't you stop_____?

Why can't you color inside/outside the lines?

Why can't you say hello/goodbye?

Why can't you clean/stop cleaning?

Why can't you sleep?

Why can't you remember?

Why can't you forget?

Why can't you trust/stop trusting?

WHAT KINDS OF...?

What kinds of conversations do you most enjoy?

What kinds of details are you most apt to notice?

What kinds of advice are you most likely to take?

What kinds of mistakes don't you mind making?

What kinds of mistakes mortify you?

What kinds of stories do you like to be told?

What kinds of stories do you like to tell?

TIP: *I take my advice sideways. I will be mortified by any typos in this book. I am always up for something funny. I want music in the stories people tell.*

WHERE WERE YOU WHEN...?

Where were you when the sky turned green?

Where were you when you laughed out loud?

Where were you when you made an important discovery about yourself?

Where were you when you felt ashamed?

Where were you when something tragic happened?

Where were you when you lost your self-confidence?

Where were you when you gained your self-confidence?

Where were you when you said, "I love you"?

Where were you when you wish you'd said, "I love you"?

WHAT DO YOU BELIEVE...?

What do you believe the holidays are for?

What do you believe you are capable of?

What do you believe is unjust?

What do you believe stories should do?

What do you believe stories must not do?

What do you believe family is?

What do you believe a home is built of?

What do you believe you are here to achieve?

TIP: *We ask questions to find ourselves. And to name our purpose.*

ON THE HUNT FOR MEMORY

Writing true requires us to write about what we remember; it also asks us to ponder how memory is returned to us. About where we go to find the past and what we do when it floods straight through us. I think a lot about memory, and where it lives. I have come to the conclusion that those who write most knowingly about the past are those who understand what it is to stay open to the tug of long ago.

"I can't remember," we all say sometimes. And then we do.

I've found my memories by walking fast through my neighborhood. But I've also found my own past in a box of letters. (*That's* what he said.) In a book of childhood watercolors. (*That's* how I saw.) In the raw burst of urgent, nearly forgotten poems. (*That's* how I was feeling.) In the face of a cereal box. (*Those* were the words that my young son read.) Along the sea at low tide. (*Here* is where my uncle was happiest.) On a crayon wrapper. (*This* is the color he said his skin was.) In a karaoke song. (Now that I remember the song, I remember the day, I remember how we laughed afterward.)

I've found memory in a very specific sunrise pink (they saved me that day), and in the circus sounds of those horseshow grounds (heralding the taste of lemons), and on the banks of a pond in winter (it was like *this* on the day I first began to skate). I've found my past when I've gone outside to watch a cardinal peck at the berries on a bush. I've found it by driving to the mountains and staying at the inn where my family stayed when I was a child.

Often memories just find us; it's true. They besiege us, blindside us, shadow us, tag us, populate our dreams. And while writing true stories is certainly a far more sophisticated enterprise than simply writing our memories down, it can be helpful (when not overwhelming) to have so much raw memory at hand.

But when we come up empty, when the past is a blank, when we are not sure, when we are bereft of *then*, when it could have been *this* or it could have been *that*, when we are fuzzy, the gig is not up. We are not done in. We will not leave the pages of this workbook empty. There are photographs, songs, artifacts, letters, landscapes to return to, a book of watercolors.

LET MUSIC TAKE YOU BACK
EXERCISE

Find a computer—in the library, at home. Search for the Gregorian chant of the Benedictine nuns. Let the music play.

Do nothing for ten minutes (at least!) but listen.

I'm betting that this music has just returned you to a parcel of your past.

Which parcel?

Write it here.

TIP: *Think of memoir as a bridge, a strut, a span connecting the known and the unknown, the distant and the near, the you and the me. Allow music to carry you back, ahead, across.*

FIND YOURSELF IN A PHOTOGRAPH

EXERCISE

Ask your parents or your aunt or your grandfather or your favorite first-grade teacher for photos of you when you were younger than you are now.

Take those photos to a quiet place and study them. Who is with you? What are you wearing? What does the expression on your face tell you about your mood?

Choose a single photograph.

Tell the story of that time and place, that version of you.

TIP: *Memories beseige us. They confuse us. They scatter us. Then they congeal. Let it all happen to you—the hard stuff, the bewildering stuff, the ambiguity, the possibilities.*

TOUCH THE PAST

EXERCISE

Search the house where you live for an object that has always meant something to you. The kaleidoscope on the mantel—a gift from the uncle you loved. The candle in the drawer that lit the holiday meal when you were in fourth grade. The flashlight that has guided you through storms. The rug where everyone who has ever visited has stood. The chest of old fabric samples that your mother collected. Your jar of buttons. The skull of the fox on the sill, the nest of the hummingbird in the bookcase, the book.

In a quiet place, sit. Allow the object to take you back to a very specific moment in time, and write that moment here.

TIP: *"Memoir is by nature a kind of meta-writing. It's partly about the sheer act of recollection, and partly about viewing the recollections from a distance, asking what shape they take, what vessels best hold them, and then rearranging and articulating the entire account in a way that reads well."* — Angela Palm

CAUGHT ON FILM

EXERCISE

Grab your camera. Turn it on. Start snapping. Take five quick photographs of the room (or the outdoor world) where you're sitting. Now study them carefully, one by one. Find a detail—the way a shadow falls, the way the dust is floating, the color of the grass, the streak in the window, the stuffy chair, the broken back of a book, the moss on the log, the spoon in the sink, the mess or the extreme clean—that recalls for you another time in your life, another scene.

Remember it all on the next page.

TIP: *In the early days of memoir we stand waist high in the sea. Our feet sink into the sand. The gulls circle. The waves slap salt against our skin. In yielding to the tug of the past, we are yielding to uncertainty.*

FIRST MEMORY

You've gone beyond just writing truths and remembering. You're not merely making lists of things that happened. You're sinking in. You're going deep. Now go back—even deeper—into time.

Find and write the first thing that you remember. Yes—the first thing. Impossible? Ridiculous? Unlikely to be true? I know. It's hard. It's shady. It's surreal. Courage is required. But look at all you've written so far. You've got courage to spare.

Elias Canetti in *The Tongue Set Free* writes that his first memory is a color: red. A. Manette Ansay in a memoir called *Limbo* says her first memory is the fear of losing memory. When Marie Arana looks back to her Peruvian childhood in *American Chica: Two Worlds, One Childhood*, she finds the poetry of sound and the distinct smell of blood. Oliver Sacks, on the other hand, looks back and finds the elemental order—and power—of metals in *Uncle Tungsten: Memories of a Chemical Boyhood*.

Color. Fear. Smell. One person. Streaming people. Interiors. Summer skies. Awakenings. Somewhere inside all of this you stand. You are smaller than you are now. More confused, perhaps, but also graced with wonder. You are alone. You are on someone's knee. Your sister is pulling you in a wagon. You hear an argument. You find a bird with a broken wing. Your uncle is taking the lid off a box of rocks. Your mother is singing. Someone is dropping a lobster into a pot. There is the smell of garlic. There is a spear of lightning in the sky. There is the rumble of a car. You are standing in the tide. Someone has covered your feet with sand. A clown has come to your house. A magician has shown you a trick. Your sister is screaming.

You're not going to be sure about most anything. But find a thread, and pull.

FIRST MEMORY
EXERCISE

You know what to do.

TIP: *The more you remember, the more you will remember.*

CRITICAL JUNCTURES

You were an only child, and then you had a brother.

Your 92-year-old neighbor was your best friend, but then she got sick.

You got lost in the forest and had to find your way.

You decided, at last, to stand up against the school bully.

You decided to stop being the school bully.

You stood up to your father when he nearly hit your mom.

You told your brother that you knew his secret.

You were tempted, but you said no.

You almost went on that trip, but you stayed home.

You stopped hoping the stray cat would find another home and brought it in from the rain.

You took the job.

You didn't take the job.

You tried out for the team.

You didn't try out for the team.

You volunteered to help.

You didn't volunteer to help.

You said yes.

You said no.

You did not say maybe.

We go right, we go left. We lurch forward, we hold back. We plunge in, or we investigate. We stand up, or we sit.

We've had plenty of decisions to make, and every single decision we've made has somehow helped us become the person we're becoming.

Critical junctures.

No two ways about this: We all face them.

Those of us learning to write the truth must write them.

YES

EXERCISE

———

Write of a time when you said yes to a possibility.

TIP: *You don't have to get this right. You just have to try to get this right.*

NO
EXERCISE

Write of a time when you said no.

TIP: *And now ask yourself: Which is the more interesting story? The yes or the no? Which one tells you more about yourself?*

REVERSALS

EXERCISE

Write of a time when you went back on a choice you made—admitted you'd been wrong, admitted you'd been weak, admitted you wanted to walk in the opposite direction from the direction you had chosen.

How hard was it to turn around on your path?

How did it feel to change your mind?

What were the consequences?

TIP: *I want to read the memoirist who is uneasy with ease. The one who doubles back, isn't sure, scuffs the page with maybes. Here's your chance.*

FAIL ME NOW

We're all to blame for something. We fall more times than we can count. We carry terrible secrets with us. Our failures feel like weights. But when we write about how we have failed, we are writing about how we are human. And when we finally look up from the page, our hearts feel lighter than they did before. We have taken responsibility. We own more of our past.

Those of us who write the truth understand that there is no true and truly meaningful story that does not honor, and learn from, adversity, mishap, or misery. "Vulnerability," *New York Times* columnist Charles Blow has written in his memoir, "is the leading edge of truth."

Hold that thought in your head. Think about all of the pieces you've written so far in this book. Ask yourself how honest you really have been. Have you shown us your true self? Have you yielded a glorious failure? Have you fallen down on the page, then picked yourself up?

It's only us right here. Dig deeper.

NOT TOO LATE FOR A COURSE CORRECTION

EXERCISE

Write about a time when you set out to achieve a goal but failed. What went wrong? How might you have corrected your course? What did you learn in the process?

Don't just write what happened.

Tell a story.

TIP: *A story isn't an anecdote. A story has actual meaning.*

FAIL ME NOW
EXERCISE

———

Write about a time when failure was the best thing that could have happened to you. When an important part of who you are today was shaped by a thing that went wrong.

TIP: *Failure is one of the best things that can happen to a memoirist. How boring it all would be if everything went according to plan.*

NAVIGATING YOUR WORLD

HOMEWARD BOUND

Memoir is about the self, of course. But it is also, equally, about the world beyond. The houses in which you were raised. The houses you built. The houses you left. The meals you shared. The landscapes that shaped you. The weather that played havoc with your plans.

Memoirists are forever writing home. They are setting the reader down in front of the family TV. They are walking us around their grandmother's kitchen. They are taking us to the far edges of a country called Sri Lanka—putting us in the garden where crazy stories get told and distorted, believed and trashed. They are sitting us down on the stoop. They are packing up the boxes of their lives so that they can trade one home for another. They are describing and defending, loving and leaving, searching for a new home, searching for the home that they once had.

Homes protect us and contain us. Home is where we know and where we are known. Home is where we can lie very still, beneath our covers, hands on our ears, listening to nothing but the pumping of our own blood. Home is where we allow ourselves to be ourselves and allow ourselves to be cared for. Home is want and need, that holiday gathering and that broken toe, the window that opens and the door that opens out.

Home is where the story begins.

But what is home? When I've asked my students this question, they have written about the car where they sing their favorite songs, the shower where they think their private thoughts, the body (with all the scars) they haul from place to place, the calm center inside a yoga breath, the family-room couch where the dog has slept, the warm peace of a favorite song, the tree they've climbed and called their own. The smell of bread, baking.

To write of a house or a home is to write of architecture, sounds, smells, personal history, neighborhood history, street names, hidden things, ugly things, beautiful things, and hints, perhaps, of family history. It is to go in for vibrancy over standard-issue facts. It is to be smart about verbs.

FAVORITE ROOM

EXERCISE

Think about your house, your actual house (or the house in which you spend the most time). Walk us into your favorite room. Write it so right that, were we to go out on a Saturday house tour, we'd recognize this room at once as yours.

TIP: *Maybe you want to go back to some of the early pages of this book to remember what you've already written about bedroom doors or private places. Build from the stories you've begun.*

BEST LOVED
EXERCISE

A wedge of light in your attic? A dark corner of your closet? A bench where you, alone, dream? A favorite stair to sit on? The window you watch for—something?

Write about the place in the house that you love best.

TIP: *I love the place where the sun is falling. I follow it, room to room, hour by hour.*

SAVED THINGS
EXERCISE

Imagine a storm coming, a fire burning, war at your stoop.

Make a list of the things you would not leave behind.

Write about what one of those saved things means to you.

TIP: *It's the question you cannot stop asking: What do you love?*

WHAT IS HOME?
EXERCISE

Maybe home is, for you, the same as house. (If so, defend the concept.)

But maybe your idea of home does not equal your snail-mail address. Maybe it's all wrapped up with the riverbank where your dad taught you to fish, or it's the park in the city where you go to feed the birds, or it's the first car of the subway train you take, back and forth, every day, to school, or it's the garden where you tend your daffodils.

Maybe home is a circle of chairs, or a library, or a long path, or a best friend, or your idea of soul. Maybe it's a dream you have, the dream you keep returning to.

Write home.

TIP: *Your ideas about home are, in many ways, proof of your ideas about life.*

DINNER IS SERVED

For many of us, the idea of home is all bound up in food. And certainly, many lasting, meaningful true stories happen over a plate of spaghetti or a steaming Pad Thai.

My mother was a talented, instinctive cook—pinwheel cookies I never understood the math of, carrots good as candy. When she was in the final stages of her final illness, I understood, a devastating realization, that I would never eat her food again.

The loss was profound. The loss remains.

What is food to you? What happens at meals, with you? How have your memories been shaped by flavors, the sound of a knife chopping, the smell of garlic, the peeling of a banana, the uncrinkling of a lunch bag, a holiday meal, a juicy apple, the loud volcanic sound of a smoothie being made, the sizzle of eggs, an excess of pepper, the smell of a freshly diced onion, the Christmas paella?

There are entire memoirs and memoiristic essays by writers like M.F.K. Fisher and Diana Abu-Jaber, Mary Gordon, Kate Moses, and Chang-Rae Lee that begin and end with food.

But what we're thinking about right now is you. We want to know what happens when you sit down in, or purely remember, jam and popcorn, silverware and tables, the food you made or the food that you were served.

THE PERFECT FRUIT

EXERCISE

What is the world's most perfect fruit? A Clementine, a strawberry, a tomato? Green grapes or purple grapes, with seeds? ugli fruit, or papaya? The humble banana?

Write a true story in which your favorite fruit stars. The time when you received the fruit as a gift, perhaps. The time when your little sister shared her last slice of the juicy green apple. The time when there was only one single bite of the apricot left, and six of you decided to share it. The time when you fought with your uncle and aunt over whether an avocado was a vegetable or fruit. The time you ate the unripe mango.

Tell the story true.

Make sure that we can, by the end, taste that fruit.

And that we know just what your true story means.

TIP: *Pay attention to the odor of things. To the collision of words and images. To the size of your own handwriting as you write into these pages.*

PREPARING A MEAL

EXERCISE

Think about the last time you watched someone making a meal or a single dish, someone scooping out the mashed potatoes in the lunch line, someone crying after chopping up the onion, someone secretly (or so they thought) licking the batter off of the cookie-dough spoon.

Or think about the time you made the dish or meal yourself.

Tell the story so well that we can taste it.

TIP: *Embrace the memory that surprises you.*

AT THE TABLE

EXERCISE

I have a student who believes that her life, her moods, her ambitions, her hopes, her faith in the world all reflect—in some way—the meals she has shared with her family. The conversations that have transpired across the table. The stories they agree to tell. The dishes they pass, one to the other.

Is it like that for you?

Or are family meals elusive?

Write about a family meal and what it means to you.

Or write about what it is to eat alone.

TIP: *"What separates memoir from nonfiction, in my mind, is that the author is an important actor in the narrative and, in reading the account, we see how, during the course of the unfolding story, the author—along with the other people, animals, and landscape—is transformed."* — Sy Montgomery

HERE AND BACK AND HERE AGAIN

———

Maybe we can't gain clarity—heroic clarity—until we step away from the place or people we're trying to write about. In order to write about our houses, for example, we may just have to walk down the street and then turn, return. We may have to play the part of strangers in our own lives. Sharpen our vision. Pay closer attention. Look as we have never looked before.

Make room for surprise.

Wait, we think, as we stomp back toward our address. There's a lamppost we'd forgotten planted in our lawn. There's a faded paper pumpkin still hanging in the window, despite the fact that it's wintertime: who forgot to take that down? There's a big clump of basil in the window box that needs some picking. The clock in the lobby is broken; how long has it been broken? That woman down the hall has left her door unlocked, unopened. Does she always do this? Have we not been noticing? And that man over there, the one who is our dad—maybe he's more tired than we ever thought he was. Maybe his lips are smiling but his eyes have lost their shine. Maybe it's time to ask how he is, and really mean it this time.

We go away from what we know to understand the road we're on, the life we're living. We learn from the distances that exist between the remembered and the known, the rumored and the proven, the here and the there, the familiar and the newly seen, the expected and the deliberately sought-after surprise.

What distance are you willing to travel so that you might clearly see?

LEAVING
EXERCISE

You are on a journey. You have left one place for another in your life. Maybe a suitcase is involved, and a moving van. Or maybe the thing you are leaving is an idea about your life, your love, your expectations.

Write about leaving. Write with the understanding that you won't remember all the details, but you will remember how leaving felt.

TIP: *"Memoir wants to test and try. It's as interested in what can't be remembered as much as what can be—but even then it's not so sure."* — Paul Lisicky

RETURNING

EXERCISE

Now write about a time of return. What do you see? What strikes you as odd about the place you thought you knew so well? What strikes you as profoundly beautiful?

Write the details of your own house (or home) that somehow escaped your daily notice until you were gone for a while.

TIP: *It's those telling details again. We're using every prod and poke to help you see your world and life.*

WE NEED SOME LANDSCAPE

———

Do you need a big-bowled sky to feel alive? Do you seek mesas, rivers, shorelines, a sentinel of forest trees, Italian hill towns, a dusty road in Africa, a view through the bushes? What happens to your mood in the company of panoramas and sweeps? Are you the sort of person who climbs to see, or will we find you crouching low? Do you look for movement, do you look for people, among the fixed features of stone and sky?

Landscapes can defy not just expectations but us, at least for a while. Landscape can leave us lost, and confused. Landscape can also call up color, emotion, memory. When we write about landscape, we are writing about how we see. We are taking note of the details that surprise or comfort us, the geography that startles or rewards us, the rush of scenes or wings, the elemental specific things that, in one way or another, tell us and others. I value this, I'm shocked by that, and this (this pool, this mountain, this back yard, this alley, this fritillary) was something I discovered, something that felt both wildly foreign and my own. We are announcing who we are, the nature of our adventures, our willingness (or not) to be mystified, lost, confounded.

KNOWN LANDSCAPES

EXERCISE

Write of a familiar landscape—of a place that you know well. Imagine me standing beside you, now walking with you, now climbing with you (I'm slightly behind, breathing hard). What are we seeing? What is your history here?

TIP: *I want color. I want sound. I want memory. I want ache. I want you to transport me.*

UNKNOWN LANDSCAPES
EXERCISE

Take a trip to an unfamiliar place. Maybe that's just down the street, where you hardly ever go. Maybe your aunt will drive you to a farm. Maybe there's a bus route that winds along a river somewhere. Grab a friend. Equip yourself with this book and a pen.

Put all the unfamiliar stuff you are seeing right here, on this page. Think shape, sound, color, texture, dimension, height, volume. Think of how it makes you feel. Think of what it would take to feel at home in this place. Tell the story of this landscape.

TIP: *There's nothing more alerting and awakening than putting ourselves into a brand new place. Look at what it does for our languge, too, our approaches as storytellers.*

WEATHERIZED

Do you stare through windows watching the skies?

Are you a storm hunter?

Are you sizzling right now in your SPF, hoping for a breeze?

Does weather star in the stories you tell?

If yes, what kind of weather?

If not, why not?

Seriously: Where is weather in your life?

Weather presses down, affects our mood, influences our daily fashion, sets our pace. We will or we will not be wearing that paint-splattered Yankees cap, that ripped-sleeve hoodie, that plastic poncho with the "Flower Power" decals (who bought you *that*?). We will or will not be dashing through raindrops, chilling in the shade, trudging through the snowdrifts, hiding out in the plain sight of a sunny day. We are social or less social according to the forecast. Torrential rains

can change our minds. Breezes can send us searching for our kites. Snowfall may leave us feeling stuck or feeling infinitely peaceful. Cool sunlight through autumn leaves can turn us thoughtful, or maybe hopeful, or, perhaps, suddenly sentimental for a long-lost afternoon.

We can do nothing about the weather. The weather can do everything to us.

As I type these words, a soft snow falls and I've got a cold tingle in my toes. Three days ago, I walked in the sun, wearing my Paint Splatter Doc Martens, no coat, no scarf, no gloves. I couldn't sit when that sun was shining—I had to walk and fling my arms and laugh. I'm sitting now, typing this—the heater blowing, my hot tea steaming, my thoughts concentrated and distilling.

How has winter shaped your life? How has it shaped your memories? How has it shaped your ideas about possibilities? Or maybe summer is really the season of you—that time of year when you feel most yourself, most unobstructed, most alive. Maybe all your best memories, your favorite songs, your most enduring stories were born within or live inside the summer months.

Weather is fact. And symbol.

THE WEATHER OF NOW
EXERCISE

On this page write the weather of right now. Go outside (unless, of course, a tornado is coming, or hurricane winds; your writing can wait, if that's the case). Investigate. Teleport us straight to the scene—the temperature, the humidity, the quality of breeze (or wind) and sky, the cast of shadows, the streak of sun, the puffiness or streakiness or nothingness of clouds.

Make it real.

TIP: *Memoir is what we find out about what we thought we knew.*

THE WEATHER OF THEN
EXERCISE

Now snatch this slice of present weather and let it take you back in time. When else in your life did the weather feel just like this? What was happening in that moment? Who was near, or who was far? How were you feeling?

What is the story?

TIP: *Go back through the writing you've already done. Can you connect the present weather with any of the memories you've written down? Can you write that story?*

THERE ARE PEOPLE OUT THERE

PEOPLE WHO NEED PEOPLE

———

By and large—though of course not always—we are not the only people inside the stories that we tell. There's usually someone else hanging around on the edges, or sitting right there, in our face, or singing "Thunder Road" in the car beside us, or shaking the maracas in our band. Joey's in the corner, laughing.

Debbie stole the shoes you were going to wear to the eighth-grade dance, and Martha stole them back from Debbie, but now you've bought another pair from Jessie, your older sister who works the Saturday shift at the Shoe Palace in the mall (and just got her first tattoo!). Jane works there, too, and the thing is that after you bought those shoes, Tim, your date, never even showed up for the dance. Weirdly, Carl from Biology did, with a burst of orange-tipped daisies in one hand and a pair of red socks tucked inside the pair of boots he borrowed.

"Carl?" you said.

"To the rescue," he answered.

Afterward, you got sick, and you stayed in bed, and your brother, Joey, who is laughing again as you tell this tale, brought you a mug of mint tea, and one week later, when you were all better, but perhaps still confused, Darby showed up at your front door—Darby, who is your best friend now, Darby, the only girl you'll ever trust when you go out rock climbing, which is so much more exhilarating—and so much more you—than all that nonsense with the dance, and you're sorry for the long sentence here, but that's sometimes how life is. Looking back, telling this now, you have to admit that Carl's red socks drilled a little hole in your heart, that you won't forget them, just as you won't forget him for being the person who reminded you that unkindness and kindness can happen at the same precise time in your life and that you have to choose how much kindness you will finally believe in.

If you are paying attention to your life, you're paying attention to the people who come and go and stay. Who they are. How they make you feel. What they teach you about the world and yourself, how they shape your ideas about friendship, trust, betrayal, love, and almost everything else.

Maybe you take some of this for granted.

You can't when you start to write your life.

But oh, how dangerous it can seem, to put another on the page. How easy to slip from describing someone to judging him, from suggesting another's motivations

to declaring that you know for sure. It's important not to blame another as we write. It's essential that we use our words to explore and clarify, which is not the same thing as using words to embarrass or condemn.

We don't write truth as an act of vengeance.

Or, at least, we shouldn't.

The best way to be kind to the people on your pages is to try to understand them. To not deflate. To not point. To not scream. To get at the heart at why they do what they do, say what they say, fail but sometimes succeed. Was your no-show Tim paralyzed by shyness? Was Debbie planning to shine up those pilfered shoes? Was Ma mad because she wants more for you, and because she struggles to give you all she hopes you'll have?

Writing the truth asks us to think deeply about ourselves. But it also requires us to think deeply about others. Just as much, and just as fairly.

PARENT OR CARETAKER

EXERCISE

Think of the person who has known you longer, or better, than anyone else. Your mom? Your dad? Your aunt? Your grandparent? A teacher?

Help us see that person—how she looks, how she dresses, how she moves where she likes to be—by remembering and writing a very particular scene.

TIP: *I'm looking for a scene. I'm demanding dimension.*

FAMILY MEMBER
EXERCISE

We don't, as the old saying goes, get to choose the members of our family. Sometimes we can't even imagine who the failed matchmaker was. Your green-eyed brother eats nothing but pizza and cheese doodles, watches TV all day long, and huffs at your organic, gluten-free diet (and your big shelf of books). Your father is a philosopher who has never ridden a bike. Your stepmother can talk of no one but herself, and she does it loudly, resoundingly, unbearably as you sit in your chair reading poems.

Tensions erupt.

Write a true story about an erupted family tension. Make room for understanding. No aimless ridicule allowed.

TIP: *There are no one-dimensional bad guys in real life. And no one, not even you, is an unflawed hero.*

NEIGHBOR

EXERCISE

We can tell stories about the fights we've had, the words we've shouted through windows, the late-night battles over petunias. But we can also talk about forgiveness, sudden friendship, the way time has erased the anger and made the garden seem silly (and now too full of weeds).

Write the story of a neighbor you came not just to understand, but to appreciate. Show us how the relationship changed. Help us see this very same person as you saw him once and see him now. What, in fact, has changed?

TIP: *In the essay "Mrs. Dunkley," the Australian essayist Helen Garner tells a wonderful story about seeing someone new (in this case, a former teacher). See if you can find a copy. Then write your own true tale.*

FRIEND

EXERCISE

What is a friend, and how do you know who your friends are? What happens when a person you trusted loses your trust, and is it possible for a broken friendship to heal?

Write a true story about either finding or losing a friend.

What do you learn about yourself and your capacity for closeness and/or forgiveness as you look back and try to assemble all of this with words? How does it help you, in crafting these words, to approach the page with openness and not foregone conclusions?

TIP: *Once I wrote an entire memoir* (Into the Tangle of Friendship) *about how the friends I've chosen have shaped who I've become. Now, all these years later, I could write the book again. I bet you have plenty of friendship stories. No need to write just one.*

FIRST BOSS

EXERCISE

I was one of those kids who was always taking a job—at a jewelry store, a library, a catering service, and insurance company (oh, the smell of those mimeograph machines; yes, I tell the truth: mimeograph machines). In every new job there were people to learn—bosses and coworkers to figure out and to get along with.

Write a story about first impressions on the job (especially first impressions about a particular boss or coworker). Then write of how those first impressions changed. And why.

TIP: *I keep asking for shifted perspective stories because that is what memoir ultimately requires. Not the static reporting on a life, but the dynamic of evolved understandings.*

NOT MY JAWN

You're in one room. Someone you know well is in the other. You know you are you and she knows she is she, but neither of you has any idea about who is sitting on the other side of the wall. You're each about to say ten phrases loud enough for the other to hear. Your mission: to speak the phrases that are most consistently you, the bits of dialogue or commentary that you are presently known for.

What ten phrases will you say out loud so that your friend will (near instantaneously!) identify you? What is your everyday-speak? How do you riff? What are your songs? What are your catchphrases?

> *That jawn belongs to me.*
> *I'm feeling full of the banter.*
> *It's a meh day.*
> *Let's reddit it.*
> *She's so rekt.*
> *I don't like posers.*
> *What's in it for me?*
> *Give me a dime.*
> *I would prefer not.*
> *Tell me something fine.*

A few pages ago we were talking about people. Who they are, why they matter, how they dress, what their histories, preferences, politics, faults, triumphs are, how we introduce them with language. Clearly we can't write about people if we don't write the way those people talk. If we don't listen for their language mix. If we can't render it on paper.

If we don't produce some dialogue.

Not a lot, mind you. Not too much—never too much. Any true story that is overstuffed with quotation marks is going to be suspect—unless you've gone around with a tape recorder (as Buzz Bissinger, in his book *Father's Day*, does) collecting every bit of conversation verbatim. Can you really remember (end to end) the lecture your mother gave you when you were four about the importance of turning off the water while brushing your teeth? Can you quote, from memory, four pages worth of dialogue you had with your grandfather on his eighty-third birthday? When your chemistry teacher went off on a riff about hydrogen, were you writing it down, word for word?

True-tales dialogue is a very tricky thing. It can't be overdone, or you'll be questioned. It can't be underdone, or your story is achey—a lonesome, sterile exercise that ignores a huge part of what it is to be human, what it is to know another, what it is to interact with our odd selves.

Your job is to take note of how people talk in a most specific way and to insert into your stories, from time to delicate time, just enough suggested dialogue so that readers can imagine the greater conversation that went on. Don't pretend you can remember every last word. Don't pretend that words weren't spoken.

And when you can't remember anything for sure, find a way to signal to the reader that you are writing your best guess about the words that might have been.

YOU-SPEAK

EXERCISE

You know those phrases I just alluded to? The ones that identify you? Write them down here, as many as you can think of. Know how you talk. Imagine how you are heard. See if any of these phrases help you improve or expand any of the true stories you've already written.

TIP: *Dialogue is about words, of course. But it is also about silences, gestures, the way you twirl your hair or touch your bald spot. Think about all the ways you communicate.*

THEM-SPEAK

EXERCISE

Now take the three people you feel you know best and make a list of their catchphrases, their idiosyncratic language twists. Record ten phrases for each. See what this teaches you about these others—and about how you listen. Best if the three people you highlight here are people you've already introduced in previous pages.

TIP: *Training yourself to listen to how people speak is like training yourself to see.*

THEY ONCE SPOKE

EXERCISE

Choose a moment from a few years ago—a conversation that you remember well that involved one of the three people you just listed catchphrases for. Create that scene on the next page, using only enough quoted dialogue to put us right there, with you, in that true space. Remember, your goal is to be as honest as possible, quoting only those things you are pretty certain were either actually said or most likely would have been said.

TIP: *I know this one is hard. I bet you want to turn the page. But stop. You can't write memoir if you don't learn how to build a scene with brief bits of remembered (or highly probable) dialogue.*

THEY NOW SPEAK

EXERCISE

Write a scene—a conversation—that happened to you just today. The words should be fresh in your head. Your ability to capture this moment—accurately—should be enhanced by your short-term memory skills. How much dialogue do you feel comfortable quoting before you start veering into fiction?

TIP: *Perhaps the heart of this story lives between the lines, in the words you did not record, in the white space you left behind.*

PERSONALITIES

Annie Dillard's mother is always, she is perpetual, she is heard. From *An American Childhood*.

> Mother must have cut a paradoxical figure in her modernist living room, with her platinum blond hair, her brisk motions, her slender, urbane frame, her ironic wit (one might even say "lip")–and her wee Scotticisms. "Sit you doon," Mother said cordially to guests. If the room was bright, she asked one of us to douse the glim. When we were babies, she bade each of us in turn, "Put your wee headie down." If no one could locate Amy when she was avoiding her nap, it was because she'd found herself a hidey-hole. Sometimes after school we discovered in our rooms a wee giftie. If Mother wanted a favor, she asked, heartrendingly, "Would you grand me a boon?"
>
> This was all the more remarkable because Mother was no more Scotch, nor Scotch-Irish, than the Pope.

In Vladimir Nabokov's *Speak, Memory*, we meet a girl named Colette. She glances up with freckled eyes.

> She would be ten in November, I had been ten in April. Attention was drawn to a jagged bit of violet mussel shell upon which she had stepped with the bare sole of her narrow long-toed foot. No, I was not English. Her greenish eyes seemed flecked with the overflow of the freckles that covered her sharp-featured face.

Calvin Trillin remembers his father as a sweet, enduring frenzy in *Messages from My Father*:

He had a large collection of marching-band albums and, when Sukey and I were children, there were times when one of them would set him marching himself. This happened rarely and spontaneously; my father did not march on command. We would wait in one room while he circled the ground floor of our house. Every time he entered the room we were in, he would be marching in a different way—one time listing precariously off to one side, the next time rolling along in a Groucho Marx stoop, the next time after that marching in a sort of hip-hop—pretending to take no notice of the fact that Sukey and I were both on the floor, helpless with laughter.

Chang-Rae Lee's mother is in the kitchen cooking, she will always be cooking. Touching the point of her knife to the white of the bone, crushing the sugar in the essay, "Coming Home Again."

For kalbi, she would take up a butchered short rib in her narrow hand, the flinty bone shaped like a section of an airplane wing and deeply embedded in gristle and flesh, and with the point of her knife cut so that the bone fell away, though not completely, leaving it connected to the meat by the barest opaque layer of tendon. Then she methodically butterflied the flesh, cutting and unfolding, repeating the action until the meat lay out on her board, glistening and ready for seasoning. She scored it diagonally, then sifted sugar into the crevices with her pinched fingers, gently rubbing in the crystals.

We remember how others spoke, laughed, walked, sat, cooked, waited for us. We put those who have mattered to us on the page.

CHARACTER DEVELOPMENT

EXERCISE

In *Between Them: Remembering my Parents*, Richard Ford suggests that "the chore for the memoir writer is to compose a shape and an economy that gives faithful, reliable, if sometimes drastic coherence to the many unequal things any life contains."

Drastic coherence.

Choose three people who have a starring role in your life, your memoir. Put their photographs right here, in these pages. Now write of these individuals in vivid detail—their crooked smiles, their ducklike tufts of hair, their half dimple, their creased forehead, their empty piercings, their tattoos, their shoulder blades, their funny knees, their hairy fingers, their disproportionate ears. Write of them so spectacularly that their photographs will not be needed in the memoir you finally write. Then edit to achieve drastic coherence.

PERSON 1

TIP: *You will know if you are doing this right if you discover, as you write, a fact, a trait, a line, a moment that you did not know you knew.*

PERSON 2

PERSON 3

TIP: *We know when we start to exaggerate. We know when we lie to make things fit or to make the story turn out a certain, perfectly symmetrical, deeply self-congratulatory way. We know when what we write won't resonate with the others who have lived their lives near us. Tell the truth. Make it matter.*

DARKROOM

TAKE A PICTURE

We've already agreed that old photographs can carry us straight back to other times, moods, seasons, and earlier versions of ourselves. We've agreed, too, that new photographs—taken just now and taken with abandon—can spark our remembering selves by inviting us to dwell on details that might hold clues to our past.

Photographs are fixed, but they are not. Photographs are about one specific second, but they can also be about the future. Photographs are personal, they are universal, they are proof of something, but are photographs the truth? Photographs can operate as metaphor and counterweight, as tease and opposition, as the other half of a parenthesis.

Here we are going to work with three kinds of photographs:

Photographs from your personal history.

Photographs from the global archive.

Photographs in and out of sequence.

In each case, you'll be searching for the truth.

THE TRUE STORY OF A PHOTOGRAPH

EXERCISE

Find a scrapbook, an album, an envelope of photographs. Choose one image. Write the true story that the photograph contains without ever referring (with your words) to the actual picture.

Now write the story again, slipping the photograph itself into the telling.

How does your story change?

TIP: *In the early pages of my third memoir,* Still Love in Strange Places, *I wrote about a family photograph and the tear that ran through the physical picture. That tear, that fracture, that fissure became a returning metaphor for the El Salvador that I was writing about. Think about the damage done to the photos you consult, and what that tells you about your story.*

DOCUMENTARY EVIDENCE

EXERCISE

———

Subtract four years from your current age. Name the year. Think back to the most important thing that happened to you that year and write the story based on what you remember.

Now go to the library (or an interesting Internet place). Search for photographs from your named year that tell you something more about the world you were living in then.

Return to your story. How can your photographically enhanced understanding of that year improve the story you've told?

TIP: *Once I heard a famous memoirist boast about how easy memoir writing was. No research required, he said. You just write what you remember. Nope. Research is required. The world is bigger and much more interesting than your own unimproved memories.*

IN AND OUT OF ORDER

EXERCISE

Grab your camera (again). This time take ten photographs within five minutes. Study the images in the order they were taken.

Write the true story that those photographs support. What do they tell you about the five minutes you just lived that simple recall would not have told you? How do they help you tell a story you might not have otherwise been able to tell?

Now scramble those photographs. Lay them out across the table (or the screen) in this new order. Write the story that might have been.

TIP: *Some of the most interesting stories are not chronologically told. In fact, that is almost always the case. Compare your two stories. What is the difference? What does that difference mean?*

WRITING YOUR MEMOIR

IT'S NOT (JUST) ABOUT YOU

Why, in the end, do we write true stories? What's in it for us—these pages of adversity and self-discovery, triumph and tarnish and gleam? And what, in the end, is memoir?

Ask any working memoirist on any given day, and, as you have seen, you'll get a different response.

Truth doesn't automatically make a story interesting. Really good true stories offer not just a series of life events but a deliberate suggestion of what it is to be a human being—to experience confusion, despair, hope, joy, and all that happens in between. The best true stories take a singular life—yours—and turn it into what I call a signifying life, which is to say a story that makes room for the reader. The best true stories recognize that the writer is not the only person in the room.

Among your many responsibilities as a memoirist is to make your readers feel seen. To not go all monologue-y on us. To not write as if your story matters more than anything that might ever happen to me. I like to encourage memoirists to focus on themes—to go beyond the anecdotes and facts themselves so as to discover binding notions about what it is to be alive. I also encourage memoirists to think about each memoir as a quest—as a search for answers to guiding questions.

- How do we survive the loss of another?
- How do rebuild our trust with someone who has hurt us?
- What is friendship, and why does it matter?
- What is normal, and is that a condition worth achieving?
- How can we heal others if we are suffering ourselves?
- What are the consequences of freedom?
- What are the politics of love?
- How well can we ever really know another?
- How do the people we know shape who we become?
- How do we release ourselves from the things that shame us?
- Can faith in beauty save us?

Write toward questions and themes.

Make your story my story.

Make me desperate to know just what will happen next.

MAKE YOUR READERS FEEL SEEN

EXERCISE

Write a true story that makes your readers feel seen, which is to say: Write as if you are having a conversation with the person who is standing or sitting on the other side of the page.

TIP: *Writers make room for the dreams of their readers.*

BRING THE WIDE WORLD IN

EXERCISE

Do you care about justice? Do you care about the environment? Do you care about kindness? What has your obsession with music boxes taught you? What have you learned from that one writer you will always read? What is the power of a garden?

Write something that teaches us as much about the world beyond as it teaches us about you. Tell this as a true story that involves us in your passions, your knowledge, your special interests.

TIP: *When you write like this, you are writing bigger than yourself. That's memoir.*

MAKE A SCENE

EXERCISE

Spend some time thinking about the big, universally relatable questions your memoir might address. Make a list of them here.

Now choose one single question and create a scene that somehow illustrates or addresses that question.

TIP: *Think of your vast attention to the words on this page as a kind of penance for the roads not chosen. Think of compensating for ordinariness with new grammar and wild rhythms.*

WRITE YOUR PROLOGUE

I like to think of the prologue as a container. As a vessel into which we place our voice, our themes, our questions, our particular way of seeing. A prologue hints at what is to come. It introduces not just the story, but the sound of the story. It augurs. It hopes. It hints. It teases. It gets us going.

In *Lab Girl*, Hope Jahren uses her prologue to talk to her readers, to encourage them to think like scientists, to view the world like she does, to participate. "So let me tell you some stories," she writes at the prologue's end, "one scientist to another."

Stephanie LaCava begins her prologue to *An Extraordinary Theory of Objects* with an assertion: "I was always strange." Just four words in, and we can already begin to guess what this memoir will be about, and how it will be told.

Patti Smith launches *M Train* with these words: "It's not so easy writing about nothing." And then goes on to show us (magnificently) how such writing gets done.

"You are what makes me indominatable and how I know to keep walking when I feel crippled in every conceivable way," Mary-Louise Parker writes, at the start of *Dear Mr. You*. The words are for her father. The words are her frame.

Finally, into his brief prologue for his memoir *My Mistake*, Daniel Menaker slips this sentence: "My brother died when he was twenty-nine after surgery for a injury that I caused." It's a devastating sentence. It is the seed from which the entire story grows.

IT ALL STARTS HERE

EXERCISE

Not every published memoir needs a prologue. But when we are writing our memoirs, when we are working on our first and second and third drafts, a draft prologue serves as our touchstone. It helps us remember what we're doing and why we are doing it. It hints at things to come, it articulates the guiding questions, the themes. It establishes the sound of the prose.

So write your prologue here. Think of this as the sacred place where you articulate the journey you are about to take yourself and the reader on. And if, in the end, your prologue is powerful and essential to the book you finally write, leave it there, at the start of your memoir.

TIP: *A prologue is not a simple synopsis. A prologue hints, suggests, evokes, tells a story.*

TIP: *A memoirist could quit at any time. Right here, for example, on the cusp of things, in the early acquaintance, before suggestions have settled in as stubborn facts. Don't quit. All memoir is a quest, to find out, first, what happened, and to find out, next, what it means.*

TELL THE TRUTH. MAKE IT MATTER.

THE STORY CONTINUES

You have done some of the hardest work there is—discovered and tested and refined your voice, asked yourself penetrating questions, remembered the places and meals that shaped you, the people who taught or loved or frustrated you, the history that surrounds you. You have moved from anecdote to meaning. You have captured the beginnings of your story inside the vessel of a prologue.

You will never, of course, know everything about yourself. You don't really know who you were as an infant child. You don't know the whole of what others have whispered about you, hoped for you, believed you would become. You don't know the whole story. You never will.

Remember, as you work, to go beyond what you readily know. To interview those who knew or know you, to spend time in libraries reviewing the newspaper headlines of your life, to pore over books about the countries you once traveled to, to sit with old scrapbooks, childhood toys, the maps that place your home or adventure within/against the larger topography, mornings spent listening to the songs of before.

Remember your life. Research your life. Examine your life. Find meaning.

And then keep writing.

TELL THE TRUTH. MAKE IT MATTER.

TIP: *Memoirists write the memoir to find out.*

TIP: *Those whose faith has faltered is a memoirist's subject. Those whose hope has paled. Those who suspect there is more to living than just living, that a juncture is not an end but a beginning.*

TIP: *Memoirists stand on the edge of the next act, wondering what the next act is.*

ABOUT THE AUTHORS

The authors are grateful to the following publications, in which fragments of this book previously appeared: the *Chicago Tribune*, the *Huffington Post*, the *Millions*, *Creative Nonfiction*, *Brevity*, and *Publishing Perspectives*. For more on the art of memoir, please refer to *Handling the Truth: On the Writing of Memoir* (Avery).

To continue the memoir journey, sign up for a free memoir newsletter, and find out more about our five-day workshops and e-learning opportunities (including our UDEMY memoir shorts), please visit www.junctureworkshops.com.

BETH KEPHART

Beth Kephart is the award-winning author of 22 books and the 2015/2016 recipient of the Beltran Family Award for Innovative Teaching and Mentoring at the University of Pennsylvania's Kelly Writers House. *Handling the Truth: On the Writing of Memoir* won the 2013 Books for a Better Life Award (Motivational Category) and was named a best writing book by *O Magazine*, *Poets & Writers*, and many others. It is an increasingly popular text among workshop leaders.

Kephart's other books include such novels for young adults as *This Is the Story of You* (Chronicle Books), a Junior Library Guild Selection, a 2016 Bank Street winner, and a VOYA Top Ten selection; *One Thing Stolen* (Chronicle Books), a Parents' Choice Gold Medal Selection; *Going Over* (Chronicle Books), a 2014 Booklist Top Ten Historical Fiction for Youth; *Small Damages* (Philomel Books), the 2013 Carolyn W. Field Honor Book; and *Undercover* (Laura Geringer Books/HarperTeen), a five-star book named to numerous Best of the

Year lists. Her novels for young adults have been translated into French, Dutch, Brazilian-Portuguese, German, Simplified Chinese, and Complex Chinese.

Kephart is a National Book Award finalist (memoir) and a winner of the Speakeasy Poetry Prize. She was awarded grants from National Endowment for the Arts, Pew Fellowship in the Arts, Leeway Foundation, and the Pennsylvania Council on the Arts.

Kephart chaired the 2001 National Book Awards Young People's Literature Jury, has delivered keynotes and lectures about memoir across the country, has written for publications ranging from the *Chicago Tribune* and the *New York Times* to the *Millions, Wall Street Journal, Salon, Philadelphia Inquirer, Shelf Awareness,* and *Publishing Perspectives,* and has led numerous writing workshops in elementary, middle school, high school, university, and community settings. She has twice been featured in large, months-long installations at the Philadelphia International Airport, was featured in the WHYY-TV show, "The Articulate," and was the June 2016 keynote speaker at the Radnor High commencement ceremonies. She is a partner in Juncture Writing Workshops, delivering five-day memoir workshops in selected locales across the country, and producing a monthly memoir newsletter.

WILLIAM SULIT

William Sulit is the co-founder of Juncture Writing Workshops. He has collaborated with Beth on multiple book projects as an artist, photographer, and designer. He is an award-winning ceramicist with a master's degree in architecture from Yale University.

JUNC | TURE
WRITING WORKSHOPS

———

www.junctureworkshops.com

CPSIA information can be obtained
at www.ICGtesting.com
Printed in the USA
LVHW111647131121
703258LV00012B/801